YELLOW ORCHID

I0201271

a poem book by

AMBER PENNIX & TYNIKA DELK

Yellow Orchid: A Poem Book by Two Friends

Copyright © 2018 Amber Pennix & Tynika Delk

All rights reserved. No parts of this book may be used or reproduced in any manner whatsoever without expressed written permission of the authors with the exception of reprints in the case of reviews.

ISBN: 0-692-16267-4
ISBN-13: 978-0-692-16267-5

Front cover photo by: Brittini Chase

First printing edition 2018.

www.amberpennix.com

ACKNOWLEDGEMENTS

A special thanks to:

Past lovers & flames
Heartbreak
Family
Friends

For without, this collection of poetry would not have been possible.

CONTENTS

Acknowledgments   i

AMBER

RED ORCHID.......1

WHITE ORCHID......11

GREEN ORCHID.......23

TYNIKA

MY BEING........32

SEARCHING.......36

THE WARNING........43

TERMINATION........49

A MESSAGE.........53

THE WAKE UP.......59

EXPLORATION.......63

YELLOW ORCHID

AMBER PENNIX

RED ORCHID

Yellow Orchid

Sometimes a soulmate comes in the form of a lover
Sometimes in the form of a mother
Or sometimes in the form of you
My friend

One day

The thought of me
Will be more exciting than the thought of them.
One day
You will see my hands intertwined with someone who isn't you
And you will realize it was me.
It was always me.

Home

Fingertips glide along my spine
Tracing every curve, dint, and line
Making me forget any insecurity that exist
Hands gripping,
Needy…As if I'm his last meal,
And boy is he greedy
Bodies become one
Ocean and water fusing into one big body
Washing away any thoughts on my mind
Other than..you
My hands reaching for heaven's skies
Your hands trying to bring yourself deeper
Into my heaven
We are one
And I
Am home

Me Before You

Sometimes when I fall I forget who I was before the trip
My mind constantly getting me & your habits mixed
Do I like my coffee with one sugar or two?
I can't remember me before you

My mind constantly getting me & your habits mixed
I wonder if this confusion can be fixed
I can't remember me before you
I want to rid of this habit & start a new

I wonder if this confusion can be fixed
You're still the first image in my head when I wake up at 6
What did I dream of before I met you?
I want to rid of this habit & start a new

You were the first image in my head when I woke up at 6
Sometimes when I fall I forget who I was before the trip
I have finally rid of this habit & started a new
Do I like my coffee with one sugar or two?...Two

Visions

I fell in love with the thought of you
But my thoughts didn't match your reality
My dreams stayed dreams, sadly

Visions of you that my mental drew
Following through with all your promises
I fell in love with the thought of you

You sold me dreams you couldn't afford to be
Marriage and long walks in beautiful valleys
My dreams stayed dreams, sadly

The venture of finding the next girl to woo
Excited you more than my love could ever do
I fell in love with the thought of you

I thought you wouldn't flee
If I loved you as hard as hard could be
My dreams stayed dreams sadly

One of the hardest lessons to be learned
Never love past what has yet to be earned
On occasions I still yearn for you and me to be two
I fell in love with the thought of you…and me
My dreams stayed dreams sadly

Garden of Love

You thought if you gave him all your flowers
His eyes would never look to another garden
But no matter how much you offered
His eyes always seemed to wander

Confusion struck you
How does he not notice all the things you do?
How could he NOT make some vow to you?
But soon you'll see
If you have to try that hard
It's just not meant to be

It doesn't make you any less pretty
It doesn't make you any less smart
Or less deserving of someone's' love & heart
Your garden just isn't suited for the soil he has to give

Remember Who You Are (An Ode to Dark Skinned Women)

Dear black sister, remember that you are the first
Remember that you are my mother
Without you there would be no other

Skin as dark as night
Without you there would be no light(skin)

Your black brothers sometimes compare you to roaches
But remember they've been conditioned by these white coaches

Taught through the media that your skin is black as dirt
But remember dirt is the soil that replenishes the Earth

Black as shit...No you're black as God
If you believe any differently than your thinking's flawed

So black mother
Skin as dark as night..Helping the light shine so bright
Remember who you are...Queen of the Earth
It's your birthright

Ghetto Girls & Boys

You are the trendsetters and don't even know it
the long nails...the way we wear our hair
all the way down to the clothes we wear
our music
our moves
even the made up words we use
we set the tone for what's in style everyday
look in the current issue of any magazine
imitating culture that for YEARS has been on our scene
makin money off what they taught us to be less than clean
let's really CLAIM what's ours
and show them who the real trendsetters are

An Ode to My Future Beau

I can't quite make out your face in the fogginess of my dreams
But I look forward to the love experience that you'll bring
I can feel your presence coming closer in my spirit
Tell me…Can you feel it?
I don't know you but I already love your smile and your mind
I haven't met you and I already want to see you one more time
Is it is possible to love someone you don't know yet?
I'll take a bet and say yes
Because the feeling I feel feels too real to be unreal
So here's to you…my future beau
I hope you look forward to meeting me
As much as I look forward to meeting you

WHITE ORCHID

To Leave??...(The Beginning)

If you wonder how someone you love
could treat you so bad
Remember to ask yourself
Why you don't love YOU enough
To leave

To Stay??...(The Middle)

To leave or to stay?
Questions I find myself asking everyday
To stay would mean having to live a life of pleasure and pain
Wondering if my love will ever be reciprocated the same
To leave would mean having to learn to live life without you
And that...Sounds too hard to do
So I guess I'll stay
And hold on to the faith that you'll learn to love me
The way I do you

I Should've Left.. (The End)

My intuition told me
But I just wouldn't listen
All the signs telling me NO
But I turned them into YES
Not knowing those "No's" were from the Universe
trying to steer me away from this mess
I chose my Mr. Right
When I should've left

Notice

Dreaming of days that have never took
A happy place
Where my mother actually enjoyed the sight of my face
What happened?
To cause my mother's love to fade
Maybe nothing
And she's always just been this way
Or maybe something
A pain she felt that cut so deep
Turning her love into the cause of my internal weep
Maybe she'll realize that I'm all she seeks
Until then I'll continue to close my eyes
And dream
That she'll notice me

Flesh & Blood

I jumped at the sound of the slammed door
And hear the shuffle of offbeat feet
The knocking makes me cover my head even more
Noises from my stomach reminding me I had to eat

Open the door baby girl...Daddy's home

My stomach turns at the sound
I hate when he speaks to me in that tone
I hate the blood that keeps us bound

Come on sweetie...I bought you a treat

Even through the door I can smell the alcohol on his breath
Attempting to give me a treat not biologically designed for
someone this petite
The sound of his words is my death

Maybe if I hold my breath long enough it won't be as painful
this time
I hear rustling signaling that the door is soon to be open
I close my eyes tight waiting for the light of daytime
How can my own flesh & blood bring me a torment this potent?
The answer being words that have yet to be spoken.

Oh, Charmer

Oh Charmer
The things you say have people
fooled.
Your intellect and looks
are used as tools
to keep us blind
from what's really used.

Make them smile and laugh.
Get them to give their last dime
just for a chance
to continue down your destructive path.

You live in denial.
Bamboozle people.
They give
you receive,
then you flee.

Just to get another fix.
Just to get another hit.

Oh, Charmer
What about your family and kids?

Responsibilities forgotten
because of the secret you hide
to keep you on cloud 9
floating above your priorities
and your past
Nothing serious,
it's all a laugh

After a while you come down from your cloud,
realizing the feeling was a lie.
Not everything's fun or fine.

Now you have to gather coins
To fix the damage you've done,
but you don't have enough change
for your name…
You feel ashamed.

Time to turn on Mr. Charmer
So he can get another hit
Trick people into believing
There's nothing wrong with him

Oh, Charmer
Oh, Charmer
Why can't you see?
Life is more than you've
Cracked it up to be

The Search

"I'll be around more"
That's what you told me countless times
Thinking back on it almost sounds like a broken record in my
mind
Used to stay up nights with pools underneath my chin
Wondering why my Daddy didn't love me then
As I got older I looked for your love in other men
Thinking if I loved them hard enough they'd stay
And when they left it almost started to feel as a routine
Maybe no man was meant to stay and love me
How could they?
The man who is half of me didn't love me enough to stay...so
why would they?
I looked for your love in other men
But now I love myself enough for you and all of them
I no longer have that pain bottled in
I now feel sorry for you missing out on the experience of me
My search for you has finally run thin

Who Knew

Who knew?
That loving you would cause so much pain
Like a soup I can't wait to taste
Burning my tongue
as soon as I let it in
and yet
I still go for another sip
~Foolish
Who knew?
That even years later the sound of your name
Would still cause by heart to spin
Endlessly
like the top record on the radio
Who knew?
That I could be so stupid
To believe that you felt for me
The way I felt for you
~Foolish

Stuck

Constantly moving but in the same place
A rat in a wheel..stuck in the same space

Moving...Moving...Moving

But somehow those thoughts still creep in
Of all the things we could've been

I try to remind myself that you didn't deserve me
My love was too pure for a treatment so dirty

Maybe I don't love myself as much as I think I do
If I did, I wouldn't entertain the thought of you

So I'll keep moving...moving...moving
Until the you're just an afterthought

One day I'll find a love worth approving
But for now...I'm stuck in the same spot

GREEN ORCHID

So Anxious (Not like Ginuwine)

I'm where I'm meant to be
But not where I want to
Accomplished so much..but yet not enough
I try to keep still and not rush
Anxious...success is close to touch
Eager to move forward and yet scared of failure
I can feel a shift coming
It's in the air..of that I am aware
I'm feeling so anxious..not like Ginuwine
Because I know very soon
It will be my time

Step of Faith

Fear of the unknown is what scares us about the dark
Because every step we have to take
is based on faith...not light
Fear of the unknown keeps us from taking a step forward
But if you keep walking
Success is around the corner
So keep the faith and move onward

Bliss

As I lay my head back down into the two day old imprint of my pillow I think of a simpler time. When the thought of my future didn't occupy my mind. Bratz Dolls and coloring books used to be what engaged me. Now the sweat from my stress can fill the tub my mother used to bathe me. Now I know why the grownups used to stress for us to not rush to get old, but they made it looks so easy. Now the thought of being on my own makes my stomach twist, like the hula-hoop my younger self loved swinging on her wrist. I guess ignorance truly is bliss.

Easy...2U

Such an easy task
Throw your food in the trash
But i don't want to be the first to get up
My anxiety has me stuck

Such an easy task
Leave a message after the beep
My anxiety makes it hard to speak

Such an easy task
Raise your hand and give your answer
You've had it since the question was asked
Raise your hand and show them that the quiet girl is the smartest
in the class

Someone faster beats you to it
Speaking the answer you've been going over in your head
And once again you're out of luck
My anxiety has me stuck

Sweaty palms and shaky knees
I wonder if I'll ever be at ease
Heart fast beating
Almost out my chest
I wonder if my anxiety will ever give it a rest

The Unknown

I don't know what the future brings,
And that's what scares me.
I don't know if I'll ever find the man that makes my heart sing,
And that's what scares me.
Will my published book even make a dime or reach anyone's eyes?
Will I ever move out of my parents' house?
Or will I be in my 30s living on their couch?

I'll be damned if that's the case.
But sometimes my laziness gets in the way.
The fear of the unknown causing me to stay in bed for just a little while longer.
The "What ifs" taking over my mind,
I guess I'll just have to take life as it comes
The high and the lows.
I can't let my fears stop me from living.
If I do then I will simply be existing as every opportunity passes me by,
Not even stopping to say hi.
Time stops for no one, not even me
So from now on I'm ridding myself of the "What ifs" and negative thoughts
This here is where my fear stops.

Future You

Sitting on the rooftop of my apartment building
Cozied up drinking chamomile tea
I'm now working on book number three

Success is now my middle name
I've even gained a little fame

Your lover comes to kiss you on the cheek
Letting you know dinners ready to eat

Every dream ever had now coming true
I know because I'm the future you

So don't worry now about what the future holds
Every goal you have...make it bold
Because soon all of them will come true
You have a lot to look forward to
Sincerely...The Future You

Selfish (All About Me)

I'm at the point in my life where it's all about me
I could care less about you
I mean I care about you
Just not as much as I used to
I'm at the point where I love myself way more than the past boys
claimed to

I'm at the point in my life where it's all about me
Confidently misplaced in life
But I know every wrong turn is indeed a right

I'm going about my existence focused on being a better me
And how can I be a better ME
if I'm always focused on trying to be a WE

Everyone should have their selfish years
Focused on shedding those hidden tears
Getting rid of past trauma and pain
So next time you love it's pure as rain

These are my selfish years
I hope yours is as fun as I plan mine to be
So Cheers
To our selfish years

To my readers,
I hope this book finds you in the perfect peace. If you're broken, I
hope it makes you whole. If you're lost, I hope it finds the deepest
part of your soul & resurrects everything that has died. I hope
these words restore.

Yours Truly,

Tynika Delk

Tynika Delk

<u>MY BEING</u>

MUVA.

she is a woman, yes
but she is a queen.
she has a great deal of experience in a lot of things.
this makes her wise.
so she helps you right, your wrongs.
she's able to make the weak, strong.
she makes the broken, whole.
she heals every hurt.
she's a nurturer by nature.
one of god's greatest creations.
a teacher, that helps with articulation, punctuation, always see
the good in bad situations
so there's no mistaken,
she will take you there elevation.
but have you ever thought all this greatness.. there's gotta be
some correlation.
because that's what i was made in.

COMPLETION.

all she ever wanted was for someone to love her.
she could never be completely happy with herself without giving
the satisfaction.

she loved hard.

she was one of a kind, rare like something in the earth's crust.

AN ELEMENT.

SEARCHING

A SUMMERS LOVE.

walking into the grocery store, and you have so many options.
chocolate, strawberry, vanilla, butter pecan, sherbet, cookie
dough.. what's your flavor?
does it excite you?
is it the type you just eat all in one day, and crave more when it's
gone?
is it the type that's been sitting in the freezer too long, so you
have to dig extra hard just to get a scoop? or
is it seemingly warm because someone left it out, but still cold
enough to save?
but stay away from that kind that everyone desires... you know
the long ones with the stick in the middle, and its gone after one
swallow.....
i know it sounds all too rewarding, but i'm looking for the type
that i'll never get tired of buying.
never get tired of trying.
because every time it touches my lips a new taste arrives on my
tongue at its finest.
so sweet that after just one serving, it'll have me extra
thirsty......
and it'll never let me down because that flavor is forever worthy.

God gave everyone a choice.
i pray i choose right.
god gave everyone a song.
thank God for your voice.
God gave us a right to choose
i pray i'm your choice.
seconds away from regret is when i feel alive
desperate to hear a lie
anxious to be broken
lost and unspoken
but till this day i thank the Lord for my curse
cause without it i would of never learned your worth.
you mean more to me than honey to a bee
you mean more to me than
a sail to the sea
you mean more to me than
sun on a flower
you mean more to me than
a king and power.

A MAN WHO LOVES.

NO LIMITS.

i want you to love me like you did you when we first met….
before you even knew you loved me,
you loved me.

A LOVE LIKE YOURS.

like cement underneath my feet.
a pool with 15 feet.
flowers that constantly resurrect.
eyes closed , blindfold because i don't want to know what's
coming next.
anchor in my soul.
don't let go, en vogue.
water it and watch it grow.
pour into me but let there be an overflow.

let's let love reach the mountain tops, and scream freely because
this is something that was destined to be.
so don't let your insecurities run you away from me.

BE MY PEACE.

the kind of love that makes me run away with you, with my cell
phone turned off.

the kind of love that makes me run away carefree from every
worry.

i want to be so used to you calling me beautiful that every
insecure flaw is buried.

when i'm used to you... i'll sleep with my hands in your briefs
but slightly on your waist.
and idk why it's just comfortable to me.

i'm not a morning person.
the drama queen in me won't let me be.
so excuse me if i'm grumpy

let's speed date every day until i know the core of who you are.
i want to take my time with you, like a monday morning.
and have no days off like i'm working overtime....

just to truly explore your mind.

ONLY ONE ARM.

2016 a year that i'll never forget.
it felt too good to be true.
it was the year i let go of old hurts for new beginnings.
new beginnings with you....
like the eleventh hour fading into noon.
may turning into june.
a flower that knows spring is coming soon.
similar to anything else that destined to bloom.
when i met you i was unsure, skeptical, and fragile.
but you protected me with layers of bubble wrap, you tightly
packed me with love and carried me with security. ensuring that
there would be no brokenness, no damage.
you see you showed me certainty, and i could tell you certainly
didn't want to hurt me.
you were for sure about what you wanted. and i loved that about
you.
you were like my favorite pair of jeans.
you know the ones that makes my booty look extra phat, and my
thighs extra thick. they fit perfectly, very similar to you.
because you were my missing piece.
and now that i have you, i can't imagine letting go.
your thoughts are the seeds of creation.
your voice is my favorite song.
your presence is like fire at my feet, and it makes my heart dance
uncontrollably.
two peas in a pod, that's how close we will forever be.
you're my best friend, that's the foundation that helped this
relationship stand.
and fading memories are footprints in sand,
so if this fire goes out, i don't want to love again.

only1arm

THE WARNING

I AM HER.

she's poison and even a drop of her will have you literally
dying for more.
and her heart was made of gold but you wouldn't know until
you start digging her mind.
intellectual conversation, she's grade A.
her body was purified, she had something wet like water.
but will give you 90 degree burn if you make her hot enough.
she had attitude.
she spoke fluently.
she loved you hard, because when y'all first hooked up there
was so much chemistry.
you were for sure you wanted her, so that showed her
certainty.
things were so much better then, now she can't help but
reminisce,
just memories.
isn't it crazy how attention is so short, your brain can only
truly focus on one thing at time?
and at that time she was what you wanted.
but some way, somehow you got distracted.
your actions, and your efforts were no longer matching.
i am she, and she is me.
deja vu, as i sit here and speak about what used to be.
never forget about our flame.
it has an everlasting burn that no one could ever tame.

*i love you, and that won't ever change, just promise me the
same. and maybe a few years from now when you've
learned to appreciate the things you have when you have
them, instead of when they're gone…
we can do it again.*

44

you saw nothing when she was right in front of you.
but every curve displayed when she walked away.

*EVERYTHING YOU NEVER KNEW YOU
NEEDED.*

THAT'S WHAT HE SAID.

"i love you still but you're not for me"

i couldn't believe what i was told.
and i had been to hell and back for this man and came out
ice cold.
and i am not for you?
you took me through things that a woman should never
have to go through.
so no, i am not for you.
i deserve someone who can reciprocate my strongest feels
and understands the love that i give.
you left scars from your actions on my heart.
you cut me deep, repeatedly.
someone who can repair the scarred tissue from where
i sacrificed my biggest part.
the thing that's dim now but shined so bright in the dark.
i hate this feeling, i wish i we never crossed paths from the
start.

i love you still, but you are not for me.

THE COLDEST WINTER.

your absence and your lack of presence
this was no a longer present, what type of investment....
was this?
things that i often i ask myself,
because they told me what you put in is what you get out,
but i made deposit after deposit while you withdrew leaving
me in the negative.
i got tired of asking you to spend time with me, it just got
repetitive.
this is no disrespecting but you neglected this,
so i have to say peace and blessings i wish you the best,
but now you turned me into a savage.

TERMINATION

we were so happy then,
i can't stop living in the past.

A MEMORY.

NOSTALGIA.

i've moved on, and i've found contentment with being
alone.
these days i find peace in my silence, but when i think of
your return my soul screams, butterflies erupt from my
abdomen.
as if i've only been pretending this whole time and waiting
on your arrival.

PROPERTY.

my body is vacant, every feeling and thought of you has
moved out.
they can tell someone has left the premises.
unwanted loved, unfilled hopes, and memories of what
used to be thrown carelessly on the corner
as if someone had just tossed everything out with no
regret at the time of departure.
there's a sign in my yard, everyone examines it when they
ride by.
looking at how amazing i am on the outside, but only
looking through the windows at the inside.
the inside is damaged, whoever was here previously didn't
understand the value of a place so sacred.
so someone has to come in and renovate.
it's too much work, so i've been on the market.
that matters less when there's a deed for my body with
your name signed in permanent marker.

A MESSAGE

trying to find another who is just like me, good luck.
she will never be.
she could never do this
i am the prototype
so you're steady trying to find duplicates,
but you could never make copies without first consulting
the blueprint.

OFTEN IMITATED.

A DECLARATION.

being in love with someone should not require changing your identity to fit someone else's idea of who you should be.

INSTRUCTIONS.

how come men never get the principle?
they never understand the underlying truth to their behavior and
it's too late to school them, cuz they'll just skip class.
but here's a little lesson
class is in session:
when i tell that i want you to be honest with me,
i want the whole truth, don't just break me off a piece like a kitkat
bar.
when i tell you i want intimacy
i don't mean sex, i mean communication, with only elevation in
secret locations, there's no time for
separation or home invasions
1+1 = 2, don't be adding no more to this equation
it can get messy when it's escalated, sometimes we need a little
ventilation.
don't ever disappoint, expectations
don't ever put your name in a shady situation, it'll just look bad
for the both of us.
i am your reflection.
so nothing but greatness is destined especially with gods
protection.
and if you're ever stressing,
let me be the one who relieves the pressure
never look for solace in another man or woman
i am your secret weapon.
as long as you have a good woman by your side, keep her.
she's the treasure buried at the bottom of the ocean.
very rare to find a good one, so once you have her don't ever
lose focus.
this is the blueprint, no coaching.
i'm hoping
that your ears are open,
and you take these words and put them in motion.
don't ever let you be the reason why a women is broken,
hopeless.

LONELY, AFRAID OF ME.

i don't even know how it feels to be alone,
is it bad that i don't want to know that feeling?
i'm scared that when it comes i'm not going to be able to
handle it or know how to manage it.
so i fill the voids with decoys that remind me of you.
and when i got tired of the imitations alcohol became my
substitute...
an epitome of addiction because people begin to associate
things they go through with what they're attached to.

THE WAKE UP

the way Christ loves is how we should love each other, but if Christ is <u>absent</u> from your life... who do you love like?

did you learn to love from your father that stepped out on your mother? or did you learn from your mother who was weak, and the only way she knew how to love was to manipulate....
that's the way she kept everyone at her feet.

NO DIRECTION.

ANONYMOUS.

it's the little things about me that he misses, he doesn't
really know who i am.

ORCHID.

you don't need to be bedded by a man with soiled hands.
for you are the only flowers that grow unwatered.

EXPLORATION

INFAMOUS.

i say your name and i smell your scent.
i picture your image and i feel your body.
the way he whisper his words.
his quiet demeanor that screams to my soul.
intangible creations, our eyes are locked and your lips
have the key.
challenge me but do not dig into my
insecurities.
There's a forest in my body with your name engraved on
every tree.
you're a part of me.

LIGHT AT THE END OF THE TUNNEL.

your smile is the sun that screams life into my body.
i want your light to bleed into my soul.

ABOUT THE AUTHORS

Amber Pennix is a Prince Georges County Maryland native, who attended Chowan University where she earned her B.A in English writing. Growing up Amber has always had a love for the arts and creating, from dancing, to of course writing. Becoming friends with Tynika Delk at Chowan she discovered they both had a love for poetry and came up with the idea to combine forces. Amber currently resides in her hometown where she is working on her first novel.

Tynika Delk also attended Chowan University with a B.A in Psychology. She is originally from Hampton, Virginia but currently resides in Smithfield, VA where she plans to continue her journey as she discovers a new found for writing.

www.ingramcontent.com/pod-product-compliance
Lightning Source LLC
Chambersburg PA
CBHW021219020426
42331CB00003B/377

* 9 7 8 0 6 9 2 1 6 2 6 7 5 *